FREEDOM

SALLY GETS SOBER AND STARTS TO GROW UP

Alexander T. Polgar Ph. D.

Sandriam Publications Inc.
Hamilton, Ontario, Canada

Freedom: Sally Gets Sober and Starts to Grow Up
By Alexander T. Polgar Ph.D.

©2019 Sandriam Publications Inc.
Hamilton, Ontario. Canada

atpolgar@sympatico.ca
www.atpolgar.com/sandriam-publications

All rights reserved.
No part of this book may be reproduced, stored in a retrieval system or transmitted in any form or by any means, electronic, mechanical, microfilming, recording, or otherwise without written permission from the Publisher.

ISBN: 978-1-9990954-2-0

Printed and bound in Canada

Cover: Workhorse Design Studio

ALSO, BY
ALEXANDER T. POLGAR PH. D.

Conducting Parenting Capacity Assessments: A Manual for Mental Health Professionals

Chronobiology: Strategies for Coping with Shift Work

Because We Can – We Must: Achieving the Human Developmental Potential in Five Generations

TWO: One Destined to Addiction the Other to be Free

This work is dedicated to all those who struggle with getting and staying sober. Because when you do, it is a great and noble accomplishment.

CONTENTS

Hi, I'm Sally And I'm An Addict 1

SALLY'S STORY

Chapter 1 Getting Sober 7
Chapter 2 Getting Unstuck 15
Chapter 3 Nowhere to Hide 21
Chapter 4 Starting Again 27
Chapter 5 Growing Up 33
Chapter 6 The Problem with Pleasing Fantasies 41
Chapter 7 Spirituality 47
Chapter 8 Sober and Moving Forward 53
Chapter 9 Reaping What I Sow 61

REFLECTIONS

About Getting Sober and Growing Up 71
Denial and Resistance 75
How We Reason 79
Getting Sober is Just the Beginning 81
Crisis 83
Transition vs Transformation 85
Status Quo 87
The Problem with the Disease/Illness Model 89
Psychopharmacological Drug Withdrawal 91

Spirituality 95
In Search of the Good 97
Other Toxic Elements 99
Not All Addicted are Addicts 101
Habilitative Experiences 103
The Paradox of Fellowship 105
Use it or Lose it 107
The Biology of the AA Fellowship............................... 109
The Benefits of Sobriety and the Pursuit of the Good... 113

Acknowledgments 119
About the Author.. 121
References 123
Sally Gets Sober and Starts to Grow Up 125

HI, I'M SALLY AND I'M AN ADDICT

I left off my life story with the above words. Words I said at my first Alcoholics Anonymous (AA) meeting. These words started a transition that I will describe in three different but very related ways. The first, is about my thinking at the various phases in the transition. The second, concerns what I did as a result of how I was thinking at any given time. And the third, is about how I felt as a result of what I did. All three are equally important, and at first puzzled and confused me so much, getting the transition started was difficult and discouraging. Drawing on my single best quality of being stubborn like a mule, I gradually overcame the obstacles in my way. One of the early lessons I learned, is that I am not a human, instead I am a "human becoming". This process is never complete. While my transition, which I now understand to be the development of my potential, is ongoing, I am at a sufficiently good place to share my experience. I hope that it will encourage some among you to stick with a journey to maintained sobriety and the realization of your wonderful developmental potential, that my words will get you started on becoming a human being.

I will describe nine phases, or parts, in my transition, from being stuck to getting on with becoming human, or developing the potential with which I was born; the two, I believe, are the same thing. The first phase was all about slow single steps forward, and many discouraging steps back. In the second phase, to get off this horrible amusement park ride, I had to learn why and how I was stuck, and most importantly, how to get unstuck. The very freaky experience of becoming unstuck and achieving sustainable sobriety happened in the third phase of my ongoing transition to becoming a human. This was a very dangerous time which could have ended tragically. Gladly it did not.

The fourth phase was a continuation of the third. To get past it required of me what in hindsight was the most courageous thing I have ever done. I dared to leave behind the safety of my AA tribe, and still remain a part of it. I no longer shared their status quo beliefs and eventually rejected their establishment views. My tenacity, that mule like stubborn streak, was really tested during the fifth phase. Not only did I have to get straight again, but I had to also do it by withdrawing from establishment intoxicants (psychiatric drugs) far more dangerous than street drugs or alcohol. Because of the damage done by this establishment condoned poisoning of my body and mind in the sixth phase, I had to first find, and then constructively use, relevant counselling services.

The last three phases I will describe are the end results of my struggles. They represent the benefits of sticking with it. In no particular order of importance, the seventh phase involved understanding and implementing the anonymously written serenity prayer. I had to learn what is in my 'power' to change and what is not. In this phase, I learned about living in harmony. Getting unstuck, and staying unstuck, - and having the tools with which to do this -consumed me in the eighth phase of my transition. I learned about who and what experiences help me to grow and develop as a person, and which hold me back. It was in this phase, I learned to read between the AA twelve step lines. Most importantly, I learned that the better question to ask is, 'what is thegood' as opposed to knowing the difference between right and wrong. In this current ninth phase, at least for now, I am finally, truly enjoying the life tasks required of me. My existence is incredibly simpler, more meaningful, purposeful and therefore full of quality since I became concerned with 'what is the good', as opposed to worrying about knowing the difference between right and wrong.

 I hope reading this part of my life's journey will provide both comfort to those of you who feel so all alone, because you are not, and then inspiration as you begin your own transition, changing what you must and can, and learning to live in peaceful harmony with what you can't.

SALLY'S STORY

Chapter 1
GETTING SOBER

"Getting sober is easy. I know people who have done it dozens of times", I often heard said - never in a really funny way, but more to be a wise ass. Until it applied to me, I had no idea what it meant. Soon enough, it became very clear that getting sober was not actually the challenge. I could easily do that for a day or two, sometimes even for a week. Staying sober, however, was the real problem. Defining 'sobriety' made the challenge even worse.

Because I was going to AA in body only, and not mind, my focus at first was on just not drinking. So, I would not drink for days, which I did, as long as I could smoke pot to escape that constantly nagging cold, unwell feeling. Of course, the pot not only mellowed me out, as I knew from past experience, it also disinhibited me, but this time not only in having sex. This time around, the disinhibition also involved having a drink of whatever alcohol was easily available. Under the influence of THC, I could always rationalize the first drink as the only one, so it didn't really matter. One was never enough though, and each episode always ended with me getting pissed out of my mind. Because of the pot, I would not even puke, so my drunkenness and hangovers were worse than ever before.

But worse than the physical hangover was knowing how I had let down all those who cared about me. To their credit, they never said anything mean but I could see the disappointment and hurt in their faces.

The worst for me was the look on my son's face. He was barely a year old, but I believed he could sense that my existing neglect of his needs was just going to continue. He seemed less disappointed in me than afraid, afraid of his mother – now this really made me feel like shit. More the reason to escape the sense of bitter cold this created by getting stoned, and then after, almost always getting drunk.

That same look on my little boy's face, regardless of how stoned and/or drunk I got, haunted me. I was on a horrible roller coaster, spiraling down and down. For his sake, I resolved to get off the ride, to remove that fearful look from his beautiful baby face.

So, for my son's sake, I gritted my teeth, stayed off pot and alcohol for a few days, and then went to a meeting. Each time this happened, and it happened several times, no one at the meeting did anything other than cheerfully welcome me. No one welcomed me back, they just welcomed me like I never left.

After several false starts, I faced the reality that even though I said it, I did not believe the first step in the twelve step AA program, that I was powerless over the effects of addiction, and that my life had become unmanageable. Since I did not believe it, I did not act it. While my words fooled others, including myself, my actions spoke more loudly and clearly than anything I said.

Fortunately, alcohol and drugs had not yet destroyed all of my brain cells and they went into action to resolve this inner conflict that was ruining my, and my son's, life.

The first unavoidable conclusion was that getting and staying straight was not something I could do for him or for anybody else who cared about me. Neither my love for them, nor their love for me, were reason enough to keep me sober. There had to be another reason, but what it was at first, was impossible to figure out. So, I listened, and I learned.

At meetings, I learned from others that I had to get and stay sober for myself. But why should I treat myself with such respect and good care? All my life I was made to feel unlovable, worthless, useless, a nuisance and an outsider who eventually lost the desire to even look in. Any possible negative label was applied to me, tramp, slut, unreliable, dishonest, drunk, crackhead, just to name a few. I was made to feel like garbage; I believed I was garbage and I treated myself as if I really was. My thinking at the time, was that garbage does not require or deserve good treatment. It simply gets thrown away and buried out of sight.

My first awakening came when someone pointed out that feeling like garbage was the same as accepting that I am a bad person. With some difficulty I was persuaded that people are neither good nor bad. People just simply are. It is their behaviour that is good or bad. Since most behaviours are learned, bad behaviours can be replaced with learned good ones, or so I was told. I didn't quite get the last part, but I sure liked the idea of being neither good nor bad. This was one of the first memories I have of feeling relieved.

The next challenge was to figure out why this 'neutral', neither good nor bad person, deserved a better life than being a disappointing shithead drunk and druggie. Not an easy question to answer if you think about it. Once again, I needed help to figure this one out.

It turned out the solution involved abandoning, dropping, this stupid word 'deserving'. On the radio news someone was commenting about a person who had been shot dead on the street, saying, "she was a beautiful, innocent person who did not deserve to die". Surely in the past I had heard similar talk, but somehow this time it struck me as an utterly stupid thing to say. I thought to myself, 'if she was ugly, and guilty of doing something bad, would she then deserve to die?" Once I thought about it in this way, it was easy to stop using the words 'deserving' and 'undeserving'. Instead, I came to accept that since it is within me to get and stay sober, that was a good enough reason to do it. Keeping it simple really helped.

Keeping it simple, especially during the initial phases, was never easy, however. At the same time as figuring out why I should do this thing for myself, I had to get my head around the reality that sobriety meant never again tasting alcohol or experiencing the very pleasant buzz from intoxicating drugs. 'Never again' was a harsh reality to accept. At first, I dealt with this harsh reality by creating fantasies that were more pleasing to myself – something of which I was very capable and had been practising ever since I was a kid.

The most pleasing of these fantasies was that I don't really have a problem, that the first of the twelve steps doesn't really apply to me. I needed this fantasy to avoid the reality that I could never, ever get high again. So, my fantasy became, "I don't have a problem, certainly not like the others in the AA group".

The creation of pleasing fantasies not only allowed me to reject the reality of being an addict, it also included other patterns of thinking that caused me a great deal of trouble. In this state (later I learned this is a stage of reasoning), I was totally into myself. My only priority was to get what I wanted, when I wanted it - and it had to happen immediately. Whatever I needed at the time was the only thing on my mind, and all I cared about, was whether or not I could get away with whatever had to be done to get it.

My shrewd planning, however, was almost always wrong. I based my rapid decisions on such screwed-up reasoning that I almost always got caught. Even worse, however, was not getting caught because that fed into my fantasy about being so clever. Those few times I did not get caught just reinforced my disastrous approach to living life.

Disastrous it was for many reasons, especially since I was making no headway. I was accomplishing nothing except making a proper mess of everything. All the things I had hated my parents for as a kid, were the same things I was now doing as an adult. It didn't take genius level reasoning for me to see that as my son got older he would feel about me as I had felt about my parents, and that he would follow in my footsteps just as I was following my parents.

These were the darkest times in my long journey to getting straight and eventually growing up. I relied on these fantasies that were more pleasing than reality, and I could not even relate to or feel comfortable with, my user friends any more.

Around this time, I took to a whole new level the creation of pleasing fantasies about myself and circumstances. I gradually, then completely, disengaged from the external world. By doing this, I literally made myself 'voice hearing' crazy. This was a brief, but awful period of time requiring its own special description at another time (in the third book of this trilogy). Needless to say, I came out of it.

Coming out of the brief but nasty dance with insanity and psychiatry, and then losing my excellent child like ability to create pleasing fantasies were the harsh consequences I faced each time I relapsed. I am the first to acknowledge now how screwed up I was; I was not, however, stupid. I could not hide from the reality of my relapses. The conflict in my mind was unbearable. How could I not have a problem and at the same time not be able to keep my word and stay sober? As I learned later, resolving this type of intense 'cognitive conflict' is the necessary ingredient to making developmental gains.

A new and better way of thinking was the end result of my conflicted mind making sense of my relapses, and the idea that I didn't have a problem while my life was a complete mess . I was unable to day dream as I used to, and I had much less capacity for harmful pretending about myself and my life. Ultimately, I lost my old exit from reality door. I could no longer create pleasing fantasies – what others called denial of my problem.

In acceptance of reality, because of my new and better way of thinking, and since I was familiar with being in a gang, or as I like to call it a tribe, I was kind of ready to try on a new tribe with its own rules, values, beliefs and required behaviour. My new tribe was going to be AA.

Chapter 2
GETTING UNSTUCK

The thinking I did to stop creating fantasies and denying my problem made me start to think about thinking. This phase in my journey was made all the more productive, as I took note of the various, so called, AA slogans constantly repeated in my group. For example, 'it ain't the drinking, it's the stinking thinking before the drinking.' I had no idea what that meant, and no one could explain it in a way that made sense to me. I kind of understood that how I thought about things, how I made sense of events, caused me to behave in a certain way. I also got that the consequences of my actions included how I felt afterward about the things I did. I started to understand that this sequence could either make my life worse, or it could make things better for me. Mostly, in the past, I experienced bad things as a consequence of my behaviour. As I said, every time I relapsed, I felt worse and then I needed to escape that feeling by getting high. It was like a horrible amusement park ride I could not get off.

At this phase in my journey to getting sober, I also had a

pretty good inkling that we addicts are a very different sort of people. However, understanding an addict as unique still didn't explain how we, especially I, reason about the world, our lives, and our daily experiences. It was something else, and that something else is that all addicts getting sober start the journey from a position of being stuck

Being 'a card carrying' member, in the past, of the user tribe served a certain purpose: it justified what I did, but clearly at a terrific price. Being 'a card carrying' member of the AA tribe also serves a purpose, a higher and better purpose than justifying my bad behaviour, but it too comes at a price. That price is staying stuck.

It dawned on me that the price we all pay for membership in a tribe is the requirement that we believe certain things, we value certain things, and we behave in certain ways. For the most part, we don't think for ourselves, instead others do the thinking for us.

As I said, I started to think about thinking. This can be a real threat to tribes, in keeping them alive, strong and in control of their members. While it may be hard to believe that I could figure this out myself, it was really not that difficult. After all, I was just exchanging the rules, values and beliefs of one tribe for that of another. While AA is a far better tribe than my previous, it is still a tribe. In spite of making progress with my sobriety, I still felt stuck, like something was not quite right. This feeling weighed on me and I felt an incredible urge to figure out what this tribe membership is all about, and what it does to a person.

Two separate, but related, events helped me to solve this riddle.

One was a memory of a psychiatrist or a psychologist, I can never remember which is which, labelling me, because of my selfish, self centered taking no responsibility and blaming others for my bad behaviour, as having a *personality disorder*. I didn't know what that meant and thought it was just an adult form of name calling for someone whose behaviour is bad. I knew my behaviour was bad, but there was nothing new about what I was doing. This was me since forever, since I could remember I had always behaved like this.

This realization about my bad behaviour having always been more or less the same over all the years, made me think of what a good and respected friend from AA had once said to me early in my sobriety. She was really frustrated with my bullshit on and off, in the program and out of it , always blaming others and never accepting responsibility. I could see she had had enough and I sure heard it loud and clear when she spat out:

"Sally, fucking grow up!"

When I put these two events together, it dawned on me that behaving like a pissy nine year old in the body of an adult either gets you labelled a personality disorder, or yelled at to grow up by those who do not call you names.

So, if I needed to grow up, it must mean that I had stopped growing up or I had gotten stuck somewhere along the way in a place that was not so good. But I was smart. I knew I was smart because I had been tested and got a very high score in what the person called IQ. My bad behaviour, even my overwhelming need to belong to a tribe, I reasoned, is not because I am stupid. I figured my childish 'personality disorder' behaviour is similarly not caused by being stupid. It must be something else, and I felt I was getting close to figuring out what it was.

Fortunately, in addition to being stubborn, I was and continue to be, very curious. This confusing problem was not going to defeat me, especially since neither alcohol nor drugs had managed to.

Putting my stubborn curiosity to work, I was astonished at what can be found and learned, all right there just for the looking. I am embarrassed to say I started with Mr. Google. I am equally proud to say, I quickly advanced to reading actual journal articles and then real, made out of paper, books.

My first discovery was a Swiss guy called Jean Piaget. He described how children reason about the rules of a game of marbles. Piaget called the reasoning, moral judgments. Reading this, I also learned about stages of development, how we can't skip any and, most importantly, how some of us get stuck at a particular stage, and continue to act accordingly, until we get unstuck. I then learned about an American, Lawrence Kohlberg, who further developed Piaget's description of stages about how people behave based on how they reason at a given stage. Kohlberg, I think, was the first to explain criminal behaviour in this way. He and some others worked in a prison for women talking with the offenders about the right thing to do in certain situations, and why. The objective was to get the women to think or reason at a higher level, expecting them to then also behave better. I learned habilitation, which means growing up, is a better word to describe what those who behave badly, including criminals, need. It is a better word, because it means people need to grow up, first in the sense of how they reason, and then, behave. . Of course, how someone feels is a constant during this process and requires constructive consideration.

There are many other smart people who have described how human beings develop. For example, Erik Erikson wrote about how over time we develop our identity or sense of who we are. I must admit many of the things I read about were not easy to understand, especially how the different ideas fit together. One point was perfectly clear: because of shitty environmental conditions, a person's development, can and often does, get stuck. I had no doubt that applied to me. The word 'shit' with which I described my circumstances applied even more once I started to understand how important a person's surroundings are..

Slowly the light went on, and it was almost blindingly bright.

After a relatively brief but serious search, I understood that I needed to grow up: I was stuck and needed to get unstuck. Being, and wanting to be, in a tribe and behaving like a pissy child in an adult's body, were all signs of being developmentally stuck, of not using the developmental potential with which I was born.

Before I could do something about being developmentally stuck, now that I was sober, I had to deal with all the problems I kept buried by getting drunk or high. I started to discover that being an addict comes with a bucket full of other issues, not just abusing substances. I would have to understand and then learn to control them.

Chapter 3
NOWHERE TO HIDE

Being sober or 'straight' for the first time turned out to be a very freaky experience. Being straight for one or two days is nothing compared to fully resetting my body to being clean after being used to having alcohol or drugs in it.. Instead of experiencing life in a way similar to listening to a poorly tuned radio station, everything was now crystal clear. Having no prior experience with true reality, this created in me some disturbing emotional states, states from which I had successfully hidden in the past with the help of drugs or alcohol.

I came to realize this too would be a challenging phase in my transition as I went through some horrible times.

The first emotional state I experienced started as a trickle but quickly became a flood; it was fear. For no particular reason, I was terrified of everything and everyone. , I felt like my very life was at stake and reacted accordingly. To be accurate, I overreacted to even the slightest sign of less than absolute support or approval of what I said or did. In frustration, people said I had anger management problems.

Perhaps it looked like that, but I was really just protecting myself from harm by being aggressive. It worked well, or so I believed, because people always backed off. It worked so well in fact, that even my AA friends, were starting to avoid me.

Being in this frequent state of fear brought back a truck load of bad memories. For example, I remembered always being afraid as a kid, sometimes even afraid for my life from a drunk or high parent, relative or friend. As I got a little older, I actually feared dying of neglect as, at my house, food money was spent on getting high. Being afraid made me an unpleasant and aggressive child, just like I turned out to be as a sober adult.

Anxiety was partner to my fear of people and events. Along with fear, I constantly felt queasy in my stomach. My mood was always sad. Later I learned that anxiety is less a reaction to anything specific, but more fear of the unknown, because I lacked the confidence to deal with virtually anything. I never knew of the need to learn so called life skills, or what one requires for living. In the past, I just didn't deal with things, instead I always chose getting high.

As you can well imagine, being afraid and also anxious about my ability to cope with any and all situations did not make me feel emotionally well. I felt, like I did when alcohol and drugs were part of my life, sad. There was an intense absence of joy in my sober life. All of these feelings overwhelmed me, robbing me of the energy I needed to do what I knew I had to, but could not.

As they say, the chickens always come home to roost. In

this case, the chickens were my habitual refusal to engage with reality once I had found alcohol and drugs. I avoided growing up by getting high. I avoided situations through which I could grow and mature by being high. Sober, I had some real catching up to do, and in a hurry. But before I could do that, I had to deal with the immediate problem of my emotions and how they were making me feel drained of all energy. If I did not deal with them, I realized, I could very well lose the support of the people who I needed the most at that time…. my AA friends.

I was in a crisis which could either turn out well or badly for me. As fate would have it, things got far worse before they got better.

The 'far worse' part of this phase I refer to deserves its own separate description. I say this because of the life and death dangers involved. Needless to say, I survived it but barely.

Here I just want to say, warn anyone going through the earliest phase of sobriety, that it will most likely put you in to a state of crisis. I don't know much technical stuff about 'crisis' but I did learn that it is a time of serious disruption to life as you had known it because you did something that upset the apple cart. I upset the apple cart by getting sober and nothing was 'normal' any more. Instead, being sober released all the fear, anxiety and sadness I had kept hidden before. As I saw it at the time, I had two choices: either I went back to my normal state of being high or drunk, give up on the AA program and go back to burying those negative emotions, or I could choose to move forward and do something about the fear, anxiety and sadness. I shared this conclusion with the person at AA who was becoming my formal sponsor. He was very supportive, said 'no problem' and had just the professional to help me. What I didn't know at the time, was that agreeing to see the psychiatrist he knew was one of my greatest mistakes, and started me on a journey from which I almost never returned.

The long and short of it is that after a very brief discussion the psychiatrist pulled out a prescription pad and put me on a "small pill" at a "low dose" that was sure to get rid of those nasty feelings.

The name of the drug does not matter. What matters is that it really messed me up. First of all, as a long term addict, I knew as soon as her drug kicked in, I was no longer sober. I was in an altered (messed up) state of mind, an all too familiar feeling, one I no longer wanted and immediately disliked. It made me feel like a hypocrite at AA meetings, but everyone seemed to be OK with me taking pills because a psychiatrist had prescribed them. They even encouraged me to stay on the pill because "it will help", especially once I got used to the weird way it made me feel.

With their encouragement I stayed on the pill. I told my doctor, however, about the weird ways it was making me feel. In response, she pulled out her trusty prescription pad and put me on a second pill that would take away the weird feelings which she explained were the side effects of the first pill.

Now I was on two prescribed drugs, feeling no pain and most importantly causing no trouble to anyone. My thinking was very different from anything I had ever experienced before, even when high. I did not care about anything. Nothing mattered, including whether I lived or died. Since I did not worry or care about anything, I did virtually nothing, and since I did nothing, there were no emotional consequences to my actions. Nothing mattered, not my son, not my family, not my friends and not my life. 'Why bother living' started to run repeatedly through my mind. And then I started to think about killing myself in a foolproof, non messy way. Fentanyl became a part of my plan.

I had a plan and I was very close to putting it into action. When I was on the very edge, preoccupied with what I was going to do, my son looked at me with his large brown, sad eyes, and now able to talk a little, said, "What's wrong mommy?". For some reason, his eyes and words shocked me back to reality. I could see that because of the doctor prescribed pills I was more messed up than ever before. It was time for me to do something about this new problem. It was time for me to once again get sober, but this time from the pills from the doctor. By then I knew how to stop drinking and getting high, but I knew nothing about getting off the pills. I did know enough, however, that I should not do it on my own. Once again, I needed help. The question was from who. To deal with this, I let my curiosity loose and started to research by reading stuff.

I was pleasantly surprised to find a sea of information. Even better, I found that I was not alone. Man, there is a lot of information out there, just for the looking and reading.

What I discovered, was that not all physicians, not all counsellors or therapists are the same. Not all buy into the establishment's ways of thinking or doing things. While it wasn't easy to find a physician to help me get off the prescription pills, it was well worth the effort. Why anyone would stay on these doctor recommended drugs is beyond me – especially once all the negative effects kick in.

Getting off the doctor's pills was terribly difficult. It was almost the same as getting off alcohol, pot and the other stuff. Much like with the illegal stuff, getting off the psychiatric pills, my mind and body were both messed up to the point that I had to go back on stronger doses every once in a while. Often, it felt like I was taking one step forward, and two steps back. Thank goodness I am a very stubborn person and eventually kicked this intoxicating habit I had formed without knowing what I was getting into. Others I met on this bizarre journey did not do so well.

Chapter 4
STARTING AGAIN

I really dodged a bullet during my nearly deadly dance with psychiatry. Funny how important lessons in life never come easy or cheap. One of the things I learned has to do with hypocrisy, a word I never used before. What it means, because I looked it up, is pretending to be righteous when you really are not.

There is a lot of that going on, including in AA. For example, it was OK in the eyes of even my, sort of, sponsor for me to be taking mind altering, intoxicating drugs because they were prescribed by someone in a white coat and they were sold to me at the pharmacy by another person, also in a white coat.

Similarly, it is OK to remain addicted to cigarettes and caffeine and still claim to be sober, celebrating it at first monthly, then yearly. This, to my mind, is really messed up thinking, and it bothered me to no end. As I was learning though, being bothered by what you hear, see or read is actually a good thing, and should not be avoided. So, I didn't and eventually my mind developed better ways of reasoning.

When it comes to sobriety or being *clean*, you either are or you're not.

I also figured out that I needed a trail guide as I got started again in my journey to sobriety. Someone objective, well informed and without emotional bias. Someone I was not likely to find among my AA fellows, especially judging by my sort of sponsor taking me to that psychiatrist for my panic attacks, anxiety, fears and sadness.

While selecting a counsellor on the basis of credentials is important, I discovered word of mouth is even better. So, I asked and asked, and got the names of some people who were very helpful to friends in similar circumstances. I also did my own selection interview before deciding on who would be my guide/counsellor.

One particular topic of conversation helped me decide. It had to do with the proper labelling of what I was going through: was the journey one of transition or transformation? The counsellor I found to act as a true guide helped me figure out that I was not in the process of transforming, or changing who I fundamentally am, specifically a person programmed by my life experiences to be an addict. This is a condition that can never be changed. I had to accept that I am an addict for life. The better description of my journey, therefore, was transition, but from what to what? Puzzling over this was very bothersome, especially since the counsellor kept on steering me away from seeing sobriety as the goal or destination of my transition.

Eventually, with the guidance of the counsellor, the

answer, which was always within me, came to the surface.

First, I had to transition from living in disharmony with who I am, an addict, to living in harmony with it and behaving accordingly. Addicts lack an internal pot-bellied stove to provide them with the heat needed to survive the often harsh, cold conditions otherwise known as life. Building this stove was a task I missed early in life, as I described before. I did not have the necessary materials, so as an adult I had to accept the reality of coping without it. Fortunately, the coping 'only' required getting the heat from an external source. This all sounds simple because it is. The challenge is in the doing, especially if you don't understand why there are certain tasks that just have to be done.

Living in harmony as an addict required regularly getting that external source of heat. When the core heat in my 'soul' was achieved and maintained I could then get on with fixing or addressing other problems.

The next lesson, of many, was that, despite regularly getting my dose of external heat, I still felt panicky, anxious, fearful and sad most of the time. I didn't feel these emotions before, or perhaps they were just bundled in with the nasty cold that comes with not having that built in pot-bellied stove. Regardless, I sure felt them as the days and weeks of my sobriety marched along. The emotions made it difficult to focus and I seriously thought about giving up my sobriety for relief from these previously buried painful feelings.

My counsellor turned out to be a short cut to research and reading. I learned that the body is connected to the brain and that we have to look after both. I knew I was not looking after my physical well being, and this was not helping my mental and emotional states.

Once again, the solution was easy, the doing was the difficult part.

The first step I took to decrease the panic, anxiety, fear and sadness was to get into shape: work out, eat better and sleep the right amount for me. I may be stubborn, but I do know my limitations, so I got a personal trainer, courtesy of my local YWCA's introductory fitness program. At first it was a challenge, but step by painful step, the rewarding benefits kept me going back for more. In better health, my panic attacks, anxieties, fears and sadness slowly got less and less intense to the point that I could tolerate talking about when, and under what conditions, either one or all of them felt particularly intense.

During the discussions with my counsellor I gradually discovered the underlying reasons for my troublesome emotions. I had them for good reasons. For one, I never acquired, through experience, any confidence in my ability to cope with life's challenges. I was constantly anxious and panicky about my ability to speak in public, to say the right thing and to know the appropriate thing to do. I was terrified of the consequences of what I was sure were to be my certain failures.

I am tempted to say much more about therapy, but I do not want this story of my life in transition to be about the ins and outs of counselling. I just want to say that in the initial phases of getting and staying sober, especially if you are considering a potential detour into psychiatry, the right guide can make the difference between success and failure. I also want to stress that counselling for me, was being actively involved in the discussion and most importantly taking responsibility to follow through with what I said I would do. I kept appointments, showed up on time, read what I said I would and did many things in between sessions to keep the process chugging along.

These incredibly difficult challenges, in my early days of sobriety, all added up to the realization that as a result of my experiences, I was transitioning from being stuck to finally developing the potential with which I was born. This was my goal, which I could achieve only if I was sober.

To keep on track, I went to AA meetings at least three times a week but often more, especially when I was feeling particularly cold. Staying alive (sober) was a necessary condition for starting and continuing to move forward in my life, including learning to manage my emotions.

Chapter 5
GROWING UP

Once I was sober again, that time from everything, including cigarettes and eventually even caffeine, it was time to get back to growing up. I already knew about people who studied and wrote about human development but simply reading their stuff did not seem to be enough. Plus, I was, more than ever before, really aware of how fragile my sobriety and state of mind were. I could not afford another relapse. I believed it would destroy me, and it would destroy whatever faith people who cared about me still had. Continuing with professional help, I decided, was not a bad idea.

I already had a good relationship with the counsellor I found after I got off the psychiatric drugs, who helped me with the panic attacks, anxiety, fear and sadness that became so overwhelming once I got sober. I asked that we spend time unravelling what is meant by growing up or being mature.

The first thing I learned was that the same conditions that prevented me from having an internal pot-bellied stove also obstructed the development of how I made sense of my experiences, what I did and then how I felt as a result. I kind of understood, by then, how this chain of events works but understanding, getting it, does not make it all better.

In the course of getting my head around the importance of environment and accepting that mine was the shits, strangely enough I got all defensive about my parents, especially my mom. I started feeling sorry for her and still hoped to make right our on and off relationship. Sometimes blaming her and Dad for what happened also was not very constructive. Alternating between feeling sorry for, and then blaming them, was bringing me dangerously close to rejecting the pot-bellied stove understanding of what it means to be an addict, and what I needed to do about it. Thankfully, my counsellor picked up on my reaction and we addressed together this emotional and reasoning problem that was pushing me to the brink, which I knew only too well, and wanted to avoid.

It did not take long to figure out that there is a big difference between blaming somebody and explaining what happened, and how. Blaming is the thing to do if someone does something bad deliberately, fully understanding the nature of the action and knowing the consequences that will follow. While there are some people like that out there, I think they are very few and far between. My parents certainly were not like that.

Mom and Dad parented the only way they knew how, repeating what they had seen and experienced themselves. They learned how to be parents from their messed-up parents. They were products of their experiences and as a result, in spite of efforts to do things better, they just kept on doing the same things. While I came to be okay with feeling sorry for both of them, I stopped blaming them. More importantly, I made a promise to stop this parenting mess from being repeated.

In response to this, my counsellor reminded me that while good intentions are necessary for change to take place, they are not enough. Action was required of me, but not just any kind. The action had to be based on understanding two things: what the developmental stages (growing up) look like, and what has to happen for people to grow.

The developmental stages I had read about emphasized the idea that you cannot skip one. I also learned that each higher stage is a better way of reasoning about experiences and that because of this, people's behaviour improves, as well as how they feel about what they did. Now it was the 'how' part of getting there I needed help with.

The help started with my counsellor explaining the difference between children 'naturally' maturing through cool and interesting life experiences and how adults like myself do it.

There are many great books on parenting which I was eager to read and put into practice with my son. In my heart I knew it was not too late to fix the mess I had made so far as a parent.

On my own, I could not find any books or information on how adult people get unstuck and get going with their development.

What I did find was about institutional, mostly jail, programs that had the proven ability to get people unstuck and growing up. Most of the programs were called 'therapeutic communities'. As interesting as they sound, I was not about to break the law and hope to go to a jail with a therapeutic community in which I could grow up. I needed another way.

Often the answer to big problems and difficult questions is the simplest one. In my case it required putting my curious nature into gear and asking the right people how to do it. My counsellor simply said, start reading stuff that makes you 'upset' and makes you think. He said without experiencing 'cognitive conflict' you stay stuck. When your mind is troubled, upset, and your beliefs and values are shaken, that's the first step to getting unstuck.

He recommended some books which I bought, planning to create a little library for myself. One of the first, and my favourite, was the book Travels, by the Jurassic Park guy, Michael Crichton. Each chapter is a description of a different experience he had. The important part for me was the way he analysed what happened, searched for the lesson to be learned and explored how else he could have behaved in each particular situation. Each time, what he was thinking influenced what he did, what he decided would have been a better thing to do required a different way of thinking.

At first, reading this book was a real challenge. Chapter after chapter, I became more frustrated and upset for a couple of reasons. First, because I had never done this kind of thinking and analysing of situations before. Second, I had never realized that there are different ways you can think about experiences. If I did any thinking at all, up to this point, I thought there was only one way of looking at things.

What sticks out most in my memory, is that even after I finished reading, because a chapter messed with my mind, I kept thinking about it. It was like a song from the radio I could not get out of my head. To my pleasant surprise, all this thinking led to a good thing. Eventually, like a light was being gradually turned on, I came up with a new way of understanding what I read, a way of thinking that was better for many reasons than what I had thought before. This new way of understanding was really exciting to me.

I could not wait to discuss this with my counsellor. He explained that the mind does not like staying in a state of confusing frustration, or as he said earlier, being in a state of 'cognitive conflict'. The mind automatically tries to fix the conflict, he said, and it almost always does this by creating new and better ways of thinking about situations. From the new thinking come different and better ways of responding. This according to my counsellor is one of the ways stuck people get unstuck, start growing up, and start to develop their potential.

There were many other books that messed with my mind, and I slowly learned to enjoy the experience. My counsellor recommended other ways of getting out of my comfort zone, by doing things I had never done before. For example, in my city the local theatre company, before opening a play, has a dress rehearsal open to the public. The cost is pay what you can. The first time I went was really strange because I had never seen a live, or any other, play before. Once I got over the strangeness of it all and paid attention to the story, it made me think far more than I ever did about the movies I was used to seeing.

Much has been said and written about the 12 steps in AA and most other self-help programs. What I don't remember ever reading or hearing is that each step is a way of getting people to think differently, which of course leads to behaving differently. Almost always, these differences are better because maturity is being created. In my case, maturity meant taking responsibility for my behaviour, how I effect others, and being concerned about the broad and long-term effects of what I do.

Incidentally, doing the 12 steps is not as easy as you might think because what is expected by each one can, and does, mess with your mind. But because the successful completion of each step is a step forward in maturity, the effort is well worth it. I recommend therefore, if you are going through the same experiences as me, help yourself out by reading what others have said about each step. Your AA sponsor can also be very helpful when you are doing the steps.

There is one aspect of growing up that requires repeating because it is key to getting, and staying, unstuck and sober. If the process of growing up lingers on, you stay stuck and there is no going forward. I am talking about the childish developmentally stuck ability to create pleasing fantasies about yourself and the world in which you live.

Chapter 6
THE PROBLEM WITH PLEASING FANTASIES

There were many tricks I used as a child to avoid the reality of what I called my 'shit life'. In TWO, I talked about sleeping, and later using mind altering substances. While I was getting and staying sober, and all the negative feelings of fear, anxiety, panic and sadness came rushing out, I briefly escaped reality by going into my head and ignoring the unpleasant outside world. Being in my head was different from creating pleasing fantasies. It was at this time that I had that short awful dance with psychiatry. This is part of my third story in this 'trilogy' of four books. Here, I want to elaborate on the dangers of being stuck in that childish stage of pretending, of creating pleasing fantasies, or as my counsellor called it, being in a 'state of denial'.

As far back as I can remember I spent a great deal of time fantasizing and playing pretend. My parents had little money and even less interest in buying me dolls or toys to play with. My entertainment came from television when my mom was not watching one of her stupid shows of fancy people just talking. What I watched was food for my imagination. Out of cushions, cardboard and chairs, I could make princess castles, sometimes even with a drawbridge. Dressing up was also a lot of fun. In my pretend world, the nastiness of home and my parents fighting did not exist.

As I got older, playing pretend was gradually replaced by fantasies about myself, my life and my future. For example, I fantasized about how smart I was, and as a result I felt no need to do homework or study for tests. I blamed my poor grades on teachers, usually using some very screwed up thinking, like they gave me a different test from what the other kids got. I truly believed in my brilliance and thought I already knew everything important. I argued about everything, always believing I was much smarter than the other person. The reality, that I pissed people off, never penetrated the shield of brilliance I created about myself.

Unfortunately, creating this pleasing fantasy life took a lot of energy and sometimes, more often than I liked, reality snuck in. When it did, it was awful, and it was these brief intense periods that got to me increasingly more. This was when I started thinking, and then accepting, that I had a shit life.

While accepting that reality was a step forward, it did not change the fact that my life really sucked. Because I could not tolerate it, I had to escape it. The use of alcohol, and later drugs, increasingly became my way out. Then I started to pretend that drugs and alcohol were not a problem, especially for me. I pretended that a person as brilliant and capable as me could handle anything. I was in charge and in full control, or so I believed.

This well practised ability to create pleasing fantasies, therefore, was a serious obstacle to getting past step 1 in the 12 step AA program – specifically the 'I have a problem' part. I would say it, and sometimes even mean it, but most often, in the beginning, my old friend fantasy got the better of me. It took advantage of my desire to be like 'other' people. People who lead glamourous television commercial lives, drinking fancy beer, wines and liquors. I wanted to be them. I was them, so I fantasized and convinced myself, this time I can handle the drink or toke, it won't go any further – there won't be a problem. But there always was a problem, each time worse than the time before.

This, in the program, then out of the program, merry go round thing I was going through was very familiar to my AA friends. Most of them had gone through the same dance themselves. So, they confronted and challenged my thinking, especially the contradictions revealed by my behaviours and the horrible consequences they produced. My mind ached after each of these 'interventions', a feeling all too familiar. Thankfully, by then I knew what had to be done. I knew I had to stop with the fantasies and find a new and better way of thinking so my behaviour could also change.

Since my counsellor was already working with me on the problem of 'growing up', I added to our sessions the problem of getting control over my well practiced ability to create pleasing fantasies.

In just one session, I learned some very important and valuable lessons.

I learned that creating pleasing fantasies is not the problem; it is only a symptom. The real problem is being developmentally stuck. My counsellor explained that pretending and fantasizing is something a kid does. It is normal for them and is one of the ways in which their thinking, creating and problem-solving abilities develop. The problem is, when someone gets developmentally stuck, they use the pretend way of reasoning: "I am not stuck. There is nothing wrong with me". This kind of thinking gets you nowhere except in trouble, and as long as you do it, moving forward is difficult, if not impossible.

So called rehabilitation of addicts who are addicted, according to my counsellor, is really habilitation by exposing them to intense experiences that mess with their minds. The more 'cognitive conflict' they experience, the more likely they are to create new and better ways of thinking. He said, this is how people develop the potential with which they are born. Grown up people, I learned, and eventually experienced for myself, cannot pretend, day dream or create pleasing fantasies. Their adult ability to see and evaluate reality gets in the way.

The goal of competent treatment programs for the addicted addicts, as for myself, is to get to a stage of reasoning in which pretending is very difficult, if not impossible. At the end of residential or counselling 'treatment' programs the best outcome is a person accepting the reality of being an addict along with everything that means. There is no cure; they just accept that reality.

I should mention here, that this kind of growing up, when it's happening, is not a particularly joyous time. It is a rather sad time. Losing old familiar 'friends' like the childish ability to pretend, is like having to say good bye to someone forever. But it is not, so I learned the hard way. When conditions in life got tough, and I was not paying attention to keeping my soul warm with the external heat of the AA fellowship, regression was quick and nasty. By regression, I mean, out of desperation to escape the present, I went back to a state of mind that was familiar and comfortable; I went back to childish pretending and creating pleasing fantasies. At its worst, I went completely into my head and danced briefly with madness.

Regression taught me to always make sure I had enough heat for my soul to cope with the nasty bullshit that occasionally came my way. This simply meant knowing how many meetings I had to go to at a given time. The more demanding life was, the more meetings I knew I had to go to. The least was three a week, but there were times when I went every day. At one time, things were so tough, I went to meetings twice a day, morning and evening. Thankfully, these times were few and far between. But when they came I knew just what I had to do. Pretending was no longer 'the boss of me'.

Chapter 7
SPIRITUALITY

As good as I was at pretending in my childish stage of reasoning, I was equally bad as I matured. I had trouble accepting the idea of a bearded god looking down, and giving or withholding the strength I needed at a particular time, or granting me a wish and denying someone else their equally important request. Since I knew so much about pretending and fantasizing, and the trouble it gets me into, I just could not buy the 'higher power' stuff in Step 2 of AA. So, I had to get my head around "a Power greater than ourselves" that is capable of restoring my sanity.

First of all, there was nothing I wanted restored. I never had sanity in the first place, that could be restored, and what I had, I did not want back. I wanted to leave my childish fantasy thinking and behaviour behind. I wanted to move forward. No, No, No. Restoring, going back, was out of the question.

Then, a Power greater than me was a problem, because prior to my sobriety, and during the beginning of it, I felt like virtually everyone had greater power than me. And, in spite of their power, authority, smarts, credentials and importance, they could do nothing for me. I had to do it for myself, by myself, while constructively using the support of others.

So, Step 2 was a problem for me, a problem I could not ignore because it was there, and by being number 2, I figured it was an important step.

My curious and stubborn nature once again ruled the day with a little help from my counsellor and AA friends. Of course, I turned to books and made a list of things I read but did not really understand. My aim, this time, was to better understand the meaning of a higher power and its importance.

For a long time, I kind of knew that adults think about God the same way children think about Santa Claus. Children believe he sees and knows everything and if they are really good, and ask very nicely, he will magically place the Christmas gifts they want under the tree. I could not get my head around how people can stop believing in Santa Claus, and then replace him with another bearded guy who more or less operates the same way. Except, instead of bringing gifts at Christmas, he grants you favours if you are really good and ask (pray) nicely.

In the program I heard things like, "God willing.... God, grant me the serenity..." and similar requests from this all knowing, all powerful guy. If he knows everything, what you need, and what you want, and he is all loving, why would you have to ask him for anything, especially asking for more of anything? Did he make a mistake, and that is why people ask for stuff? None of this made any sense to me, but clearly many people find great comfort believing God is looking in on them, listening to their requests (prayers) and then to their thanks for having a wish granted.

This led me to wondering who made up what Santa Claus and God look like. It was easy to find out that Santa Claus's famous red suit and white beard were made up by some artist for a Coca Cola advertisement. It was harder to find out who made up what God as person looks like. But I did find out. It was the artist Michelangelo, and the picture he painted is still on the ceiling of the Sistine Chapel at the Vatican, in Rome, Italy. I truly believe that when people pray to or think about God, they're picturing that bearded, half naked guy reaching out to Adam on the ceiling.

This also did not make any sense to me.

I wished I could just accept this bearded, Santa Claus like guy and be done with it. It would have been so easy to not think any more and just settle into the comfort zone others seemed to be enjoying.

Unfortunately, my curious mind, coming out of the fog of stuck development and ignorance from being stoned all the time, could not be satisfied by this childish, Santa Claus like story.

Then I got to thinking, how could Michelangelo know, how could anybody know, what God looks like, or is like? God is a pretty big idea, and requires far more brain power than I have, and probably Michelangelo had, to come up with. So, he settled, and most other people settle, on someone who looks a certain way. Too bad and so sad, that they then became so proud, of their made up picture and story, that they actually believe they have the brain power to understand this complex idea of a god

Eventually all this troubled thinking of mine got me to accept that my mind is too weak to figure out this higher power god thing. I had to come up with something else, something I could get my head around, believe and be comfortable with.

This then led me to thinking about spirituality. Christian religious books and writings were not very helpful in explaining it. It seems like it is just another comforting word, especially when someone can say, "I am spiritual".

Thankfully (I am careful not to say "Thank God"), quite by accident, I stumbled upon the First Nations people's idea of spirituality. It is beautifully simple. Spirituality, for them, means living in harmony with oneself, with others and with the environment. Of course, there really is much more to this definition, but for me, at that time, it was like a very, very bright light just came on.

Until I started on this journey of getting and staying sober, I was living in absolute, total disharmony. In addition to creating pleasing fantasies, I was pretending to be just like a person who has a warm pot-bellied stove. I believed I had the ability to make my own heat, when I could not. As a result, I was constantly freezing to death in the cold blizzard that was my life. The freezing to death, for me, was escaping my constant negative feeling by abusing drugs or alcohol. I literally died a thousand deaths.

So, rather than trying to get my head around this higher power idea and trying to figure out why believing in someone like God was important, I decided instead to accept that we everything is connected in this universe, and that fighting this reality creates disharmony, which leads to bad things. Accepting and going with the energy of the universe (sort of a Star Wars like force) was what I decided to do.

Just making this decision felt like a huge relief, like a heavy load was lifted off my back. I felt energised, and empowered to make the transition from living a lie, to being real about who I am. For the first time in my life, the slogan "the truth will set you free" made absolute sense.

The analogy often used by my counsellor, that a person without a pot-bellied stove is like an alligator who needs an external source of heat to survive, also made absolute sense to me. Regularly going to meetings no longer felt like a chore, or imposition on my time. It felt like I imagine an alligator feels like bathing in the sun, quite wonderful. Most importantly I got to this realization without hanging on to, or going back to, a childish belief in an imaginary person looking down on me from somewhere out there, granting or not granting my requests (prayers). What a wonderful feeling to know I have always had, and continue to have, everything I need, or will ever need, for a quality of life that I define and choose for myself.

Last, but by no means least, this idea of spirituality that

I borrowed and then put into practice, also made it easier to work through the AA 12 steps. Since 6 of the 12 steps make reference to God or a Higher Power, you can see how important it was for me to get my head around this higher power idea.

Chapter 8
SOBER AND MOVING FORWARD

Part of being curious is being observant, especially of people. It also includes having the confidence and/or courage to admit to not understanding or knowing why, in particular, some people behave in bizarre ways. Early in my sobriety and getting into the AA program, I was dumbstruck by what long time sober people said and did. Some people referred to them as "dry drunks" and I even heard of a book, "Sober but Stuck" that explains these strange sober people and their often awful ways of thinking and behaving.

This time, even before I started reading, it was pretty clear to me that these "dry drunks" are people who remain developmentally stuck. Somehow, they were able to admit to having a problem, but sobriety was the only benefit they were receiving from the AA program. They were only attending meetings, and therefor getting the external source of heat, but they were not working the parts of the program through which development occurs. It was troubling to hear their 'home spun', often sanctimonious, self righteous views of the world and justification for their actions. Sometimes, they reminded me of the people I drank and did drugs with. Except they were sober.

I promised myself, this was not going to happen to me..

I decided, the place to start understanding behaviour in general, had to be figuring out this business of what the right thing to do is, in situations in which one person wants one thing and another, something else. Surely, I thought, all sober grown up people know how to do this.

Sadly, what I discovered is that some grown up people, even the ones I considered 'straight', have very strange and interesting ideas about what the right thing to do is.

The most bizarre right thing for people who are stuck to do, is because some important and powerful person said so. It's like the saying "Might Makes Right". Life for them is simple. All they seem to do, is what they are told by somebody important. Otherwise, they do very little thinking. They seem to be like robots and not thoughtful at all.

Then there are the impatient ones, those who want what they want, when they want it kind of people. There seem to be many of them. They are concerned only with themselves, and what they can get away with. For them, the right thing to do is whatever they want, including stealing your stuff if you are stupid enough not to look after it. I remember thinking that this sounded like this me during my intoxicated days, along with the fantasy that I deserve special treatment (like being allowed to get away with taking things that aren't mine) because I am special.

In my AA group, most people's idea of the right thing to do, is not what one important powerful person says, but what the program says. There are a lot of references to the program (the Big Book), and very little of people thinking for themselves. The program tells you what to believe, what to value and what to do. I guess in the past, thinking for themselves got them into so much trouble, they are happy to go along with their AA tribal rules. To me they are like very religious people which, come to think of it, AA is almost like, or maybe even is, a religion itself.

Being more the curious kind, and not inclined to readily 'drink the Kool-Aid', I got to thinking, how else do people decide what the right thing to do is? Reading about this, I learned that a society, made up of all kinds of groups, can prescribe beliefs, values and behaviours which apply to everyone in that region of the world. After the tribal way of reasoning, the better way to decide the right thing to do, I learned, involves figuring out what will benefit the most people. This way of thinking is about the "greatest good for the greatest number". I was pretty satisfied with having this as my goal, and as a good definition of what it means to be a grown-up person.

Then, probably just to mess with my mind, I read about another way of thinking and behaving as a fully mature person. I learned a new word, 'principle', used as 'being a principled person' or 'living by principles'. Sometimes principles were also described as 'the good' or going for the good in what we do.

What is involved in wanting to do the good, or the principled, thing, when deciding what to do, was not easy to understand. Even now I struggle with this whole idea, but at least now I know where I am trying to get.

I am doing pretty well with this part of growing up, because I no longer worry about doing the right thing. Now, almost always, I worry about being principled, because then what I do is also good. And this question of, what is the good, means always treating everyone, and I do mean everyone, in a fair way, regardless of who they are, or the situation at the time. Sounds simple, but not that easy to do all the time. The more I do it though, the easier it seems to get. When I do it successfully, I sure feel like a grown-up person.

What helped me to understand, and at times, actually behave in a principled way, was seeing life as a sports event. Each side wants to win, but they can only win by following the rules. Applying the rules equally is playing fair, and playing fair is always being principled.

Applying this idea of 'the good' to relationships, to work, either as a boss or a worker, to how I treat everyone, including myself, has made life much easier than before. Before I schemed, wanted to have the upper hand, and always wanted everything my way. It did not matter that my way mostly produced short lived, not very useful benefits, as long as I got what I wanted. In contrast, focusing on that question of, what is the good, was like finding the key to the door behind which I was a locked-up prisoner.

On the hunt for ways to successfully grow up, I also discovered that managing what life throws at you is not that difficult, especially if you live by some basic principles. Being kind and considerate to people, regardless of who they are, is always the good way, or the principled way, in any situation.

I can't say that figuring out what is kind or considerate was easy for me. Never having experienced being treated with kindness and consideration, how was I supposed to know how to do it? But eventually I learned the skills, and they became part of what made me feel like a grown-up person.

Since I am still working on it, I don't want to say too much, but I will say being kind is similar to being principled. In other words, treating everyone in a fair way, regardless of who they are, or what the situation is at the time.

My understanding of being considerate, is to make the time and effort to get to know someone enough, to be able to have a pretty good idea (guess) how he or she will respond, especially emotionally, to a situation or my actions. Most people call this empathy. Even if I don't have the time or opportunity to get to know a person, I can still be empathic or considerate, just by thinking about how a situation or what I do, may affect their feelings. If I believe my action will harm or make another feel bad, I will not do it.

Does developing this way of thinking actually stop me from doing certain bad things? Absolutely! That is the whole point of being kind and considerate. Grown ups do not harm others just to gain something, or to get their own way. Stuck, childish people, like I used to be, do.

Last, but not least, growing up, I discovered, involves developing the ability to think for myself. Instead of having others tell me what to value, believe and do, the challenge is to decide for myself. That was not as easy to do as it sounds. Until achieving sobriety and deciding I want to grow up, I was kind of lazy and content to be stuck, without even knowing it. It was easy just to go along, follow the crowd and have others decide things for me. For example, I am still embarrassed to remember buying some dress just because the sales clerk said it looked good on me, when really it did not. Another time I bought something because the sales clerk said everybody was wearing it. Maybe I was looking for a sort of school uniform for adults, but I think not. I was looking to fit in, regardless of what it cost, like selling myself to feel like I belonged.

During this difficult transition time, it became very clear to me that everywhere you look, people are trying to make you behave in a way that mostly benefits them, not you. Buy this, go there, donate to my cause, see my movie, hear my song, read my book, buy these shoes, buy this dress and, most troubling, join my tribe.

This brings me to AA, which is not unlike a religious group with all kinds of references to God, what to believe and value, and especially how to behave. AA even has its own bible called the Big Book. For some people it is very comforting and makes life easy. Before, I thought I lived the easy life but it actually turned out to be a harder way to live. I decided to stop taking the easy way out and start exploring another way of living.

Once I got into it, it was very rewarding. The best example was my approach to working the 12 steps. Instead of accepting a step as it is written, my approach was to figure out what benefit each one is intended to produce. Just doing this - thinking for myself- I realized, was a way of growing up.

While comforting, the sense of belonging and selling the benefits of belonging to a tribe, comes at a huge personal and, I started to realize, social, cost. Because it causes so many problems world wide, I decided to write separately about this. So now, my trilogy has turned into four books. Oh well.

In the process of satisfying my now much appreciated curiosity about why some people behave so badly, by doing a lot of reading and thinking, I discovered that growing up is about achieving the potential with which I like everyone else, was born. I learned this was the way to a better life, here on earth, as told to us by all the prophets, including the Reverend Martin Luther King Jr., in 'I Have a Dream'.

Being observant and curious, and always being taken to books, is a wonderful thing. I highly recommend it.

Chapter 9
REAPING WHAT I SOW

I really like the saying that I used for the title of this last chapter. It means harvesting what you plant, and then being nourished by it. It is at the heart of taking responsibility, by understanding that life is what we make it, regardless of how badly it started out, when we were dependent on others for survival. I did not ask to be an addict, a person without a pot-bellied stove, but since I am, I have come, slowly but surely, to realize it is, and always will be, up to me to do something about it. It has been some time now since I accepted this responsibility, and I have benefited in many ways from it.

I am writing this chapter therefore, in the present time.

In listing the benefits of getting and staying sober, I want to start with a huge lesson I learned, listening to the safety instructions on my first airplane flight. The flight attendant said, "when the oxygen mask comes down in an emergency, first put it on yourself, before you put it on your young child". What I understood from this is, passed out you are no good to anyone.

With this in mind, I will begin to describe all the benefits sobriety has brought me.

Simply knowing the aim, or reason, for growing up, to eventually achieve my developmental potential, made life much easier. I'm not saying that now I am a grown up, principled person, or behave like one, even most of the time. What I am saying, is that now I know what to compare my behaviours against. Also, I now know what an important part my thinking plays in what I end up doing. For example, if I am thinking badly of someone, or I don't particularly like a person, that is when I am most likely to treat them badly. The bad behaviour could be as simple as being late for a meeting, or not doing something I said I would. Now I know that showing disrespect in these ways, is unfair and unkind, and comes from how I think and feel about myself, and the person. Those negative thoughts and feelings turn into bad behaviours, and then I feel like shit for being a shit. Most of the time now, I treat myself and all people, regardless of who they are, and regardless of the situation, with the same amount of respect and kindness. Now, I very seldom feel badly about how I treat others, because most of the time, I treat people well. Since I respect myself, I no longer allow myself to do, or say, things that make me feel badly about myself, either at the time, or later. It is really very simple.

This work I'm doing to treat everyone with equal kindness and respect also frees me up from all the troubles that come from scheming. As I mentioned before, scheming to cheat or get the better of someone takes a great deal of work. It used to make me feel tired most of the time. I no longer scheme, and I now have a lot of mental and physical energy left at the end of the day. Plus, and more importantly, I now feel better about myself.

During the most important early years of my life, I never experienced empathic nurturing. This idea was central in the first book TWO. Nor did anyone ever teach me how to be empathic. Before getting sober and starting to grow up, I did not even know what empathy meant and how important it is, particularly when parenting, but also in virtually every interaction.

It wasn't too hard to learn that empathy involves accepting another person, for example your child, as separate and different from who you are. Because the child is separate and different, the child has different likes and dislikes, feelings and reactions, from you. I know all this sounds a little mumbo-jumbo complicated, but it's not really, once you get your head around the reality that your child is not you, or some extension of you.

I learned that the best part of getting my head around this idea, and I had to be sober to do it, was the incredibly positive effect that putting it into action had on my child and me. First, my son started to feel special because I was treating him, as special. Second, because I have started to figure out what he likes, what is important to him, I am glad to give it and he lets me know how much he appreciates it. He and I have both benefited from the effort.

The positive consequences of treating my son this way made me want to do more, and to do it better. I decided I needed help, and then I went about finding it.

It turned out that such help is available, although you do have to look for it. It helps to know what it is that you are looking for. Mr. Google was very helpful in telling me that attachment disorder therapy is what I was looking for. Once I found it, I also learned that without sobriety and getting my own shit together, I would not be much help to my son in overcoming the negative consequences of how I had parented him while I was using.

Recognizing and breaking the chain of my family's history of being 'fuck ups', is a huge positive benefit of getting, and staying, sober.

There was far too much negative history between Johnny (my son's father) and me. Sober or not, there was no way that we could ever get back together. But both of us being sober, we now recognize that while separated, we are still parents and we can each work to be better at it. Because sobriety freed both of us from being stuck at that adolescent/child like self centered way of looking at our situation, we are now able to act like adults are supposed to. We are both able to look at what is in the best interest of our son, not what I or Johnny want, which often in the past included hurting each other. Starting to think and act like developmentally mature adults is a huge emotional benefit for all of us, in our little family of three.

While I am most certainly a product of what I used to

call a shit life (environment), believe it or not, even my messed-up parents and grandparents worried, maybe even lost sleep, over my dangerously bad behaviour. I made their already miserable lives even worse, when I was messed up. Now they no longer have to worry about me, or my son. This seems to be making their lives a little better. At least in their last few years, perhaps they can now have some peace. Seeing them this way also makes me feel better and gives me more motivation, if that's possible, to continue on my journey of growing up, of developing the potential with which I was born

Part of growing up, I am happy to report, includes the ability to be in an adult romantic relationship. With Johnny, I was escaping and expecting him to rescue me. In reality, though, I was not escaping I was just changing locations: my parents' place for our crappy place. Because Johnny was very much like my messed-up parents, he could not rescue me. Not because he didn't want to, but because he could not.

Now I am in a very different relationship for very different reasons. I am no longer escaping, nor am I hoping to be rescued. I am sharing my life, the good, the bad, and the ugly parts, with someone who values me enough to take the trouble to understand me for who I am. Not for who he thinks I am or wants me to be, but for who I am. This comes from the scars he has from his past experiences, which, like me, he openly acknowledges as awful. Instead of denying it, or creating pleasing fantasies about his youth, he accepts the reality of it and is now doing something about it. We are growing up together, supporting each other and most importantly, learning to care for each other by being kind and considerate.

The incredible, positive experience of being in this relationship, is not only a huge benefit of sobriety for me, but also for everyone in my social circle, especially my son. Even now, after this short time, I am seeing real, positive changes in him.

Needless to say, I am now gainfully employed. Not part time at several jobs, but full time, since I am now reliable in every which way. There looks to be a promotion in store as a team leader, and then who knows what.

One especially pleasing benefit of getting sober and starting to grow up, is that no one has, for a long time, said to me, "Sally, fucking grow up". I am thinking that's because I am growing up. I am also thinking that label of "borderline personality" would no longer apply. I am very pleased about that.

Last, but not least, the benefits of sobriety, and the growing up that comes with it, have given purpose and meaning to my life. From what I have read, this is probably the best possible way to live life. The purpose and meaning of my life, is to work on achieving the potential with which I was born. It starts with recognizing that potential as a gift, and then honouring it. As I am developing my potential, growing up, my purpose and meaning includes breaking the chains of the past, by deliberately working to be a better parent, romantic partner and person in general. I could not have done any of this without sobriety.

There are many more benefits I could list that have, and continue to, come from sobriety. I hope the few real important ones are enough to inspire, or as the counsellors say, motivate, you to work on growing up, to honour the gift of potential life gives you.

I think it's best to end this story here. The future looks bright, and I am confident in my growing ability to handle the dark spots that are sure to come, some sooner than later. I do want to remind you that during this journey, there was a short and very dangerous dark period, which I call my brief, nasty dance with psychiatry and their intoxicating tools, otherwise known as medicine. Spoiler alert, I was lucky, and I survived it. In case you find yourself in a similar situation, I have written about the experience in a separate book. While I survived the experience and 'medicine', others have not. To avoid being a victim of yet another establishment sanctioned organization, you should read the third of four books in my trilogy.

Reflections

ABOUT GETTING SOBER AND GROWING UP

Writing in the voice of Sally in this second, of four, books in the trilogy of her life is starting to be less of a challenge than it was at first. Nevertheless, it remains a challenge. The effort, however, can be justified by the importance of the message revealed in her story. Of course, her story is really a composite of many stories, and the message is directed at two targets. The first target is the Sally's of this world, and the message for them is one of hope about what can be accomplished with even a pinch of curiosity and persistence. The second target is everybody else who may be concerned about a particular person with 'addiction' issues or is generally concerned about this devastating problem. The message for all of them, is that becoming optimally informed is not only essential, but also the prerequisite to being hopeful about what can be accomplished through understanding. Once we acknowledge and define addiction as a problem of our collective creation, of adverse environmental conditions, we can then go about preventing it from occurring in the first place. As well, the same understanding can empower us to do what must be done to bring it under control when it does occur.

Once we significantly reduce, or perhaps even eliminate, the demand for intoxicants of every kind, the supply will cease to exist.

While on the topic of supply, it is important to acknowledge that there is an endless array of scholarly works about addiction, and people writing about their personal experiences with it. The intent of this four book trilogy is not to add yet another perspective to the vast body of work, but to offer a synthesis of decades worth of various explanations of this global problem . While I know the best lessons, especially about life, are gained through experience and shared through stories, as Sally is telling it, the academic in me cannot resist the compulsion to elaborate on what Sally had to say in this second book.

I ask therefore, for your indulgence. In return, I promise to be brief, to avoid as much as possible, the use of jargon and show offish complex ideas. Most importantly, I promise to restrict the elaborations to that which is relevant to each chapter. After all, there are two more installments coming, which should be sufficient for addressing most, if not all, of what is required to understand how addicts are created, how their needs can be constructively met, and most importantly, how to prevent the problem from occurring in the first place. Hopefully, there is truth about the importance of repeating that which is at the core of an important message. And hopefully, you the reader, will tolerate the repetition, because I do not intend to stop doing it.

DENIAL AND RESISTANCE

There are many obstacles to the development of our cognitive potential. Adverse environmental conditions are the obvious ones, but there are more subtle obstacles less well understood. The subtle ones are the actual ways people reason when they are at either of the two stages most of the world's population has always been, and continues to be, stuck.

On very good days, of which there are few, most of the world's population is stuck in the tribal reference group cognitive developmental perspective. The price we pay for this will be the topic of the fourth book in this trilogy. Suffice it to say here, a primary requirement of being in a tribe or reference group, is to remain stuck at this stage of reasoning. This is accomplished through some very simple, but extremely powerful, tactics that include, but are not restricted to: being told what to believe, value, and how to behave. The primary reward for subscribing, is enjoying membership in the group with all its various benefits.

On most days, however, the majority, under siege from the constant demands of life, regress to the hedonistic cognitive perspective of the stage prior to the tribal reference group one, where it is all about the self and the immediate satisfaction of any and all needs. The hallmark of this stage perspective is the ease with which pleasing fantasies can be created. And, you guessed it, the pleasing fantasies mostly are about the self. Since the fantasies are pleasing by their very nature, a person cannot see, let alone begin to acknowledge, the existence of any problem, especially that of being developmentally stuck. Technically we call this denial, the consequence of which is resistance to doing what is required. Sally hopefully conveyed well how difficult it is to get past this and get down to the business of doing what needs to be done.

In progressive, well informed community or residentially based 'substance abuse treatment' programs, the singular goal is to remove siege conditions and provide a habilitative environment. When done well, cognitive development advances to a stage at which the creation of pleasing fantasies is very difficult, if not impossible.

Getting to this stage is always a challenge, likewise staying there. Initial sobriety/abstinence can be experienced like siege conditions and the fragile advanced stage perspective can quickly crumble.

Sally, like most, during the initial phase of abstinence seriously struggled. People often regress and relapse. Many, however, persevere and get past the one step forward and two steps back initial phase of abstinence. The best strategy for most is buying into, without necessarily understanding, the need to attend 90 meetings during the first 90 days of sobriety. Being super heated internally, gets them through that initial treacherous and rough point in their journey.

HOW WE REASON

Nobel laureate, Daniel Kahneman, eloquently argued in Thinking, Fast and Slow, that, in spite of our pleasing fantasy to the contrary, the data shows overwhelmingly that we almost always do not, I repeat, do not, consciously reason, invoke beliefs, take into consideration values, make choices and through this process, decide what to do. Instead, most of the time we act "automatically and quickly, with little or no effort and no sense of voluntary control" (Kahneman, 2011, p. 20).

While this effortless fast thinking could be a survival instinct, or simply the product of learning, there is, however, a significant underlying process that is developmentally determined. Simply, cognitive developmentally advanced individuals think fast differently than those who are stuck at earlier stages of reasoning.

The difference is created by the structure of their cognitive developmental perspective.

Sally, barely out of the pleasing fantasy creation stage, like most, had not consolidated the next stage's structures. This takes more time than to merely understand the greater utility of higher stage reasoning making the state of sobriety/abstinence quite precarious. Cognisant of the fragility of just maintaining sobriety, the AA program relies heavily on its 12 step traditions. Each step, as a habilitative experience, is conducive to changing the structure of reasoning that determines how a person thinks fast.

There is no known data to support this assertion, but my experience has been that most decades long abstinent addicts are also cognitive developmentally advanced individuals, possessed of considerable emotional intelligence with which to negotiate the vagaries of life. After years of sobriety, their way of thinking fast is vastly different than it was at the beginning of their journey.

GETTING SOBER IS JUST THE BEGINNING

All addicts alter the state of their mind and body for good reasons. They want to escape from the constant, pervasive negative physical, mental and emotional states that come from not having a warm pot-bellied stove at the core of their soul. As described in TWO they are like cold blooded creatures and without an external source of heat, remain in great discomfort, which culminates in death (i.e. the use and abuse of intoxicants). But addicts have discomforts other than cold, which were suppressed by intoxicants. They come to the surface when sobriety is achieved and maintained.

The discomforts range from anxiety, sadness and fear, to obsessive ways of trying to feel better. With initial abstinence, one or more of these negative states almost always comes to the surface. As novice abstainers, just barely out of the immediate satisfaction of needs stage of reasoning, most addicts are extremely vulnerable to the allure and promises of biologically based psychiatry. As was their recently past habit, they want a quick fix and most psychiatrists are all too willing to provide it through their primary intervention tool – a psychopharmacological pill.

Sally was lucky to have escaped and survived the involuntary intoxication which was perpetrated on her.

Many others have not been so lucky. Describing this highly dangerous dance is the topic of the third of four books in this trilogy. Suffice it to say here, just because an intoxicating mind and body altering drug is prescribed by a physician, it does not mean that an addict can continue to call herself sober or abstinent. Sally certainly was not, and to her credit, dealt with it in short order. As will be described in the next book, withdrawing from the so-called legitimate drugs was no easier than it was from the illicit ones – perhaps even worse.

CRISIS

A brief word about crisis seems to be warranted, since it is the overarching state that results in people getting, and working to stay, abstinent.

In Chinese script, crisis is written in two symbols: one depicts danger, the other opportunity.

By definition, a crisis is a time when normal routine, managing life's demands, is disrupted. Sobriety for an addicted addict and indeed those addicted, certainly is a disruption of their routine, and therefore most often, a time of crisis.

The danger for newly sober addicts lies in restoring the routine, escaping either with a physician prescribed 'legitimate' drug, or an illegal buy on the corner. The opportunity in their crisis comes from finding better ways of solving the problem. For Sally, the better way involved creating a way of understanding her condition – the absence of a pot-bellied stove - and doing what was required to compensate, getting the external heat from the AA fellowship. That is to say, living in harmony with who she is.

Of course, all of this is far easier said than done.

TRANSITION VS TRANSFORMATION

Words matter all the time, and every time. While, sometimes, the sloppy use of a word can be funny, like in saying influenza as opposed to influence, most times, using the wrong word can be a problem.

Using transition to describe Sally's journey was deliberate. Using transformation or transcendence would have been, at the very least, inaccurate or incorrect.

Sally did not transcend, rise above something, nor did she transform herself from one thing to another. What she did do, was transition from one cognitive developmental stage to another, and from not knowing, to knowing, how to compensate for the absence of a pot-bellied stove.

There is no cure for the Sally's of this world, nor for any of us who has suffered any degree of childhood trauma. Without a suitable time machine and the ability to change history, there will always be a consequence to the harm we have sustained. We can, however, find better, more adaptive ways later in life to manage the negative consequences, of the adverse conditions to which we were exposed as children . Sally is a prime example of how this is done. The millions in her fellowship, learning to manage being an addict starting in the late 1940s, have paved the way.

STATUS QUO

The forces that maintain the social, cultural, economic and obstructed human developmental status quo seem to me, similar to the complex systems that maintain the homeostatic balance in our bodies. This complexity, however, should not be relied on as an excuse to continue studying the problem, instead of actually doing something about the problem now. While many variables in play a role in maintaining the status quo, probably the most significant is our inability to recognise that we are developmentally stuck, because we are developmentally stuck. This riddle, I believe, impedes understanding most of the prophet's message about our potential for a better life here, not after we die. As a result, and in spite of the incredible efforts of many people, most notably the prophets, we remain stuck. I consider myself therefore, to be in good company and not at all discouraged by their, and my, failure, so far, to convince people that being cognitive developmentally stuck is a real and serious, very debilitating problem. I have chosen to believe in the premise of Malcolm Gladwell's Tipping Point, and will carry on until that critical mass is reached, and we finally get on with achieving our full potential.

When we reach that point and recognize the problem, my experience gives me confidence in our ability to solve it. And we have Steven Perkin's Enlightenment Now as supportive evidence for such optimism. As he points out, at excruciating length, once we identify a problem, we are extremely good at solving it.

Solving the problem of being stuck includes taking into consideration that stuck people do not like others who get unstuck and upset the proverbial apple cart. No wonder getting, and then staying, sober is so difficult and fraught with multiple missteps. In reality, it is in the best interest of few people for Sally to succeed. As a dysfunctional addicted addict, she served significant economic and social purposes. So much more reason the successful Sallies of this world deserve our admiration when they get past the gauntlet of obstacles, as they transition from one stage and state to another.

THE PROBLEM WITH THE DISEASE/ILLNESS MODEL

Words matter, I say, and will continue to, indefinitely. Words are like the data we input into our computers. We all understand the axiom: "garbage in, garbage out". So it is, when we use words/concepts that are not relevant to the context in which they are applied. Because most people use concepts, such as disease or illness, when thinking and talking about addiction, the consequence, as to be expected, is that associated issues such as anxiety, sadness or fear also are considered to be medical problems.

Being an addict is not an organic disease or illness. Talking about it as if it is, leads to all kinds of wrong beliefs or expectations. Not the least of which is that it can be cured, and a person can go back to consuming intoxicants without resumed detrimental consequences. Anxiety, fear, sadness and/or panic attacks also are not organically based diseases or illnesses. Treating them as such, and most people do, can have disastrous outcomes. Since physicians treat medical problems, at least in theory, it made perfect sense for Sally to seek assistance from a medical professional when she started to experience the troublesome emotions she had been able to avoid by being drunk or high.

It did not even cross Sally's mind that the physician prescribed pills were just different kinds of intoxicants than the ones that she bought on the street corner. As with the street drugs, so the 'legal' ones also come with their own price. The price started with her not even realizing that she was being intoxicated, and that she continued to suffer the various negative physiological and psychological effects of the psychopharmacological drugs. Peter Breggin has written extensively about this along with a host of others, alas to little avail. Medicalising non medical/organic conditions continues, and in fact is expanding at an alarming rate. For this very reason, the third book in this series focuses on this issue extensively.

PSYCHOPHARMACOLOGICAL DRUG WITHDRAWAL

In most communities, there are alcohol/illegal drug detox facilities. There are no such facilities for coming off prescribed psychopharmacological drugs. Moreover, few physicians know how, or are willing, to supervise this potentially dangerous process. To her credit, Sally was able to accomplish the withdrawal on her own, with a little professional help. Perhaps having experience withdrawing from the illicit drugs was of benefit to her. Many do not fare as well, as documented in the literature and litigated as malpractice suits in the courts. Peter Breggin again is a good reference source for those with the curiosity of Sally.

Reportedly, the sedative benefits derived from psychopharmacological drugs are brief. Getting used to taking one can be a markedly difficult experience, as is getting off one or more of them. Since many have addictive qualities, even gradual withdrawal can have debilitating consequences, sometimes even life-threatening ones.

When they seek psychiatric help, Sally, and others like her, find themselves in a far more dangerously intoxicated state than they were when taking illicit drugs. As a result, their transition from one stage and state to another is unnecessarily delayed –for some, the delay turns out to be fatal. The worst of it is that they are being intoxicated (drugged) without really understanding what they are agreeing to when filling a psychiatric prescription.

Counselling, best known as talk therapy, continues to have an unwarranted questionable reputation, and for the most part, the method is significantly misunderstood. It does not help that it has many labels, including but not limited to, psychoanalysis, psychotherapy, cognitive behavioural therapy, motivational interviewing and the one to which I often resort, the identification and understanding of demons within. Once you know and understand them, they are easier to control.

I believe virtually every person, at one time or another, could benefit from one of these intervention modalities, especially people like Sally. However, at the initial phase of abstinence, when learning how to constructively work the AA program, the critically relevant intervention first required is information or knowledge. The challenge therefore, is to find a therapist, not necessarily an "addictions counsellor", but someone who thinks outside the box. Someone who does not subscribe to the medical model of addiction being a disease or illness. The best bet for anyone in Sally's position, is to find a counsellor who buys into the conceptual model advanced in this four-book trilogy. I say this fully cognisant of the apparent explicit bias of doing so; apparent because I do not believe it to be self serving, in so far as I intend to inform in the best way I know how. My intent is to be part of the solution, rather than the problem. And being part of the solution requires being fully cognisant of the context in which lives are lived. Being cognizant of the context requires curiously asking questions about it.

Much more can and should be said about the importance and value that can be derived from counselling that is relevant to the problem being addressed. Suffice it to say here, that to find a counsellor who is competent, compassionate, empathic, knowledgeable and most importantly, 'simpatico' with you, is not easy. However, when you connect with one, it will be clear the effort was well spent.

The Human Developmental Potential

Virtually all humans are born with the gift of cognitive developmental potential. Unfortunately, few are fortunate to live in conditions that are conducive to its optimal development. What optimal conditions look like was described, albeit not fully, in TWO. Robert's family was pretty good at it. Sally's family was not.

Once sober, however, Sally's life gift of cognitive developmental potential became fully available to her. Nevertheless, being available, although necessary, is insufficient. Habilitative experiences are required, and at the core is the mind's instinctive creation of new and better meaning, when confronted with conflictual information and/or experiences.

One can, through the course of working the 12 steps, or addressing issues with their AA sponsor, experience cognitive conflict and come out better for it. Alternatively, under the guidance of a skilled counsellor, one can deliberately pursue and engage in various habilitative experiences. Always, the process requires challenging existing values, beliefs and ideologies. It also requires debriefing after experiences, with the view to become consciously aware of all aspects of a situation. I often prescribe Michael Crichton's book *Travels* to model this process.

SPIRITUALITY

Spirituality, the goal of living in harmony with one's self, environment and others is the key message of all prophets. Spirituality was never intended to mean embracing religious faith, or believing in invisible ethereal spirits, including a fanciful heavenly or miserably painful afterlife.

For Sally, and people like her, living a spiritual life means living in harmony with who she is: a person without a warm pot-bellied stove, in need of an external source of heat. Living differently, as if she has a pot-bellied stove, is living in abject disharmony, and more often is a source of great misery.

Since virtually all people are born with the gift of cognitive developmental potential, to have this obstructed, or to not know that it must be activated, also is to live in significant disharmony.

Sober but stuck addicts are prime examples of the misery that comes from continuing to be stuck when primary obstacles (intoxication) to developmental potential are removed. The same misery is evident when non addicts live in disharmony, ignoring a significant essence of being human – having a developmental potential that needs to be activated.

IN SEARCH OF THE GOOD

Most accept the cultural socialization of children as a critical component to parenting. Much has been written about raising or parenting children in this regard. Of note, are books such as Raising Good Children', by Thomas Lickona and Kids are Worth It, by Barbara Coloroso. There are many others. The critical point is that parenting responsibilities do not end with teaching the difference between right and wrong. As Sally discovered, one can justify a wrong behaviour as right, from a cognitive developmental perspective. By way of example, for a Nazi, it was possible to justify all kinds of atrocities as right, because they were prescribed by their tribe. A reference group. Stage 3 perspective is one way of claiming the right. At Stage 2, another way of claiming it, is that stealing a car is justifiable because the victim left the keys in it, and therefor deserves it.

Once the fundamentals of right and wrong are integrated, the by then adolescent's socialization has to transition to focusing on the good. This is a difficult concept to comprehend, simply because you have to be close to it to do it. You have to understand and accept the benefits of promoting social harmony, before you can promote it.

To elaborate on what this means, is beyond the scope of this work. Besides, many have done this far better than I. See, for example, the work of John Gibbs and Martin Hoffman. Suffice it to say here, knowing that you are searching for what is the good, is an excellent place from which to start, once you have integrated knowing the basic difference between what is right and Detoxification

The physiology that is important in any discussion about an addicted addict, is that the body habituates at various rates to the presence of a foreign substance or chemical. The body gets used to being intoxicated and wants to maintain this homeostatic balance. Similarly, the individual (I am careful to avoid saying the mind) gets used to being stoned and, as the body, wants to stay that way.

Altering states is never easy. It takes time and effort to become a stoner, and it takes time and effort to go back to not being one. Getting there and leaving is especially dangerous for some..

To minimize the dangers of leaving there, of going back to a non intoxicated homeostatic state, it is advisable for most people to sign into a detox facility staffed by personnel specifically trained to assist.. Unfortunately, beds available in these places can be scarce, and some planning is required.

Even more planning is required for detoxing from prescribed psychopharmacological drugs, or so called, medications. This was Sally's most trying time when getting sober and is an important topic in the third of four books in this trilogy.

OTHER TOXIC ELEMENTS

People, places and situations can often be more toxic than prescribed or illicit drugs. David Hawkins, for one, has written extensively about this. I frequently recommend his book to people like Sally, who are trying to minimize blizzard-like conditions, caused by people or situations, especially when just getting sober.

Being aware, however, while necessary, is not at all sufficient for people to disengage from toxic elements. People, places and situations that suck the life from their core can be so integrated into their lives as to be the necessary norm to maintain. At the top of the toxic list, are family dynamics, how parents treat their offspring from infancy to adult states. Similarly, friends and acquaintances can be toxic, especially if they continue to respond to the getting sober and growing up person as if this transition in their life was not happening.

The most realistic strategy therefore, is the old harm reduction one. Instead of setting the goal unrealistically high, to complete disengagement, the more realistic thing to do, is to reduce contact or exposure. Above all, the realistic approach is not to expect toxic others to change. Expecting them to change would be like going out in a blizzard without an overcoat, for the newly sober and growing up person.

Some situations can also be toxic and are best avoided, especially during the initial phase of abstinence. Sorting all this out is not easy. It starts with awareness and continues with evolving strategies. Change is fully integrated when the abstinent person, like Sally, no longer feels the need to prove she is tough by willfully exposing herself, especially to toxic people, but also situations.

NOT ALL ADDICTED ARE ADDICTS

This subtitle represents a critically important distinction that makes a world of a difference in every which way. Throughout this trilogy, I have been purposefully using the concept 'the addicted addict' and writing that all addicts invariably (I do mean invariably) become addicted to one thing or another.

In contrast, we are all vulnerable to becoming addicted, even if we have a pot-bellied stove. All it takes is the repeated consumption of a substance that alters our physiological homeostatic balance, as well as our emotional state. This is the fate of many amputees, for example, who receive morphine to cope with the acute pain caused by surgery.

Other examples of non addicts becoming addicted can be found in work environments in which the culture constantly pressures one pint, which quickly becomes more, after work. Certain occupations in which the consumption of alcohol is a pervasive practice in their after-hours club can also easily lead to a loss of control, that is to say, becoming addicted.

The 'treatment' required for the pot-bellied stove

addicted is quite different than for the addict who is without one. These are the people often referred to as gaining and maintaining abstinence without ever going to an AA meeting. This is logically coherent since they do not need an external source of heat to survive. What they need, is environmental engineering and, in my experience, total abstinence for the rest of their life.

I do not know of any literature that makes this distinction between being an addicted addict and being addicted. Therefore, I cannot refer you to any readings that would elaborate on this experience-based theory. However, I do urge anyone with the curious energy, such as that of Sally, to empirically test the notion, and report to us all the findings.

HABILITATIVE EXPERIENCES

There are some very alarming social and educational trends that have even reached institutionalized status. The most disturbing of these is the creation of cognitive conflict free zones in some post secondary educational institutions. These are places in which students can hide and be assured that they will not be assaulted with different beliefs, views and cognitive perspectives than those they currently hold and which give them great comfort.

In essence, this is the perfect formula for obstructing the cognitive developmental potential with which we are all born.

Without cognitive conflict, paradox or challenge of existing beliefs, views or values, nothing but stagnation happens. In contrast, when the mind becomes conflicted by paradox or challenge, it cannot abide by being in this state. It automatically goes into solving the cognitive conflict by creating new, and always better, meaning or interpretation of experiences.

Fortunately, Sally is innately curious. She researches a problem by reading far and wide, ponders what she discovers, synthesises the information and solves the bothersome problem by creating a new, better perspective about what she experiences.

Therefore, while the cognitive conflict is initially unpleasant, the upside each time, is the sheer exhilaration, the joy, of creating a new and better way of interpreting the world. Through these experiences, Sally unleashes her developmental potential, and puts to rest forever her fear of being troubled by different points of view.

THE PARADOX OF FELLOWSHIP

There is a real paradox in embracing the life sustaining benefits of the fellowship AA offers. Because it is a tribe, while it gives life,, it also obstructs development beyond the Stage 3 reference group/tribal perspective, which is half way up the sequence of stages in our developmental potential. To belong, and thereby benefit from membership, the requirements of any and all tribes are simple. They are: subscribe to the beliefs and values of the group and behave as is prescribed by the group. The rewarding comfort of membership, however, comes at a price. The price is being developmentally stuck. And being developmentally stuck is living in disharmony with the developmental potential nature has given us all.. In essence, not living a spiritual life.

To solve this problem, like all problems, first requires recognizing it. Second, it requires the creation of a unique, individually specific strategy. A strategy that allows one to benefit from the external heat provided by the fellowship, but moving beyond the group's prescribed beliefs and values. Sally did an admirable job of this as, for example,

105

moving from a Sistine Chapel or some other type of personified deity, to embracing the notion of spirituality defined as living in harmony. In so doing, while benefiting from the fellowship, she avoided continuing to be stuck at the reference group Stage 3 perspective.

The elaborate examination of developing the ability to 'think for yourself' is the topic of the fourth book in this trilogy.

USE IT OR LOSE IT

For those of you who like a little science in your explanation, or are quick to find fault with a metaphor, there is a possible physical basis for the absence of a pot-bellied stove in addicts.

The idea comes from what is known as synaptic pruning. It is the elimination of unused synapses (connections between neurons) during a period of rapid brain development. In the analogy of the pot-bellied stove, the absence of activation (making a pot-bellied stove) with empathic nurturance signals to the rapidly developing brain that the function (stove) is not needed, and therefore can be eliminated. Once eliminated, it cannot be returned. It is lost for the duration of that person's life.

This happens in several areas of the developing brain and has been well documented in the neurosciences. To understand, requires knowing some very simple facts.

At the time of birth, the human brain consists of roughly 100 billion neurons in the cortex. During gestation and the first two formative years of life, the weight and size of the brain increases at least 5 times from where it began. This is due to an exponential increase in synaptic growth.

To keep pace with the energy required by this rapid growth, connections (synapses) that are used least, or are not activated, are simply removed.

This conservation of energy is believed to be dependent on external stimuli (Craika & Bialystokb, 2006). Moreover, the synaptic pruning for specific functions occurs at 'critical' times in the developing brain when the child is highly receptive to environmental stimuli (Drachman, 2005).

The benefit of this early pruning process is the conservation of energy. Since the brain requires 20% of the body's energy, but makes up only 2% of its weight, that which is not used or activated, is treated as a wasteful use of space and energy. Therefore, without consideration of the future needs of the individual, what is not used or activated, at or by, a critical time is treated as useless.

An addict, therefore, without a pot-bellied stove remains the same for life, and must behave accordingly to survive.

THE BIOLOGY OF THE AA FELLOWSHIP

For those of you so inclined to wonder, and curious to know, there is probably a biological reason as to why the AA fellowship serves as an external source of heat for those without a pot-bellied stove.

The biological explanation is based on some simple facts. We evolved as social pack animals and, to various degrees, our very survival depends on being part of a herd. In fact, historically, there was no such person as a true hermit or isolated individual. Perhaps there are now, but probably not.

Because we have a human brain on top of our reptilian brain we are capable of complex emotions. This new brain, also known as the limbic brain, is what makes us emotional, and in turn, social mammals.

The benefits of being social mammals are significant. It allows us to work cooperatively with each other, an ability that serves us just as well now as it did when we were hunter gatherers at the dawn of our existence. It is what gives us our parental love instinct, and what used to involve the whole village in raising each others' children.

We need to connect with each other in powerful ways for survival. Some of our kin looked out for predators while the others hunted and foraged, and especially when they slept; sleep being necessary as the time when, among many other functions, the body repairs itself.

The analogy of the pot-bellied stove is that in the limbic brain, the brain that controls the powerful impulses of the reptilian brain (most of the time), the ability to emotionally connect with each other is compromised by relational trauma, specifically failed attachment with a primary care giver.

Because it is compromised, there is a constant pervasive negative state (represented by being cold, in the analogy), which serves as a powerful drive to seek relief, the quickest and easiest way being escape through the consumption of some mood-altering substance.

The AA fellowship serves as a super saturated, extreme connection to others, because of perfect intimacy among members. Perfect intimacy in this context, is defined as congruency of feeling, thinking and behaving. This is achieved because no one has a pot-bellied stove, everyone feels lousy without it, and all know that being together, as it was for our ancestors, is necessary for survival. Everyone therefore, is on the same page, an occurrence that is rare for most of us, but when experienced, is quite powerful and rewarding. This is something we can all relate to having experienced, even those of us with a pot-bellied stove, albeit not as often or with the same regularity, as AA members.

For some, having this experience available daily, if required, as many as three times, at morning, noon and evening AA meetings, is the up side of being an addict.

THE BENEFITS OF SOBRIETY AND THE PURSUIT OF THE GOOD

The benefits of sobriety and actualizing one's natural cognitive developmental potential are vast. To describe them all, to do this topic justice, would require far more than is possible in the context of this four-book trilogy. Reluctantly, but out of necessity, I will restrict myself to listing the most important ones, but in no particular order of significance.

Life not only becomes different, but also better, for people like Sally. In pursuit of the good, instead of constantly scheming how to take advantage of others and situations, decisions are easier and long-term outcomes are always better.

With sobriety/abstinence, and activating one's natural developmental potential, a myriad of improved relationship possibilities emerges. Most noteworthy is, parental relationship 'do overs' are no longer a constant necessity. Instead of harbouring unrealistic expectations that the addict's parent, this time, will be empathically nurturing, the sober addict can learn to have realistic expectations of the parent, and avoid the invariable destructive disappointment of each encounter.

Another benefit of development involves recognizing the importance of empathy, and then deliberately pursuing its acquisition. It is never too late to learn it, and by so doing, it's possible to be a significantly better parent, spouse, friend, colleague or co-worker.

Of course, physical health also invariably improves with abstinence. This includes the brain's ability to do its incredibly complex job. Problem solving abilities improve, and with each success, people like Sally learn to see challenges as problems to be solved rather than avoided by getting high.

Each higher stage of reasoning also disproves the adage 'ignorance is bliss'. As the sober addict's world broadens, so also the cognitive developmental potential advances proportionally. Much has been written about this in the context of therapeutic communities, in which the benefits of cognitive conflict are enhanced by incrementally exposing participants to ideas and experiences way out of their comfort zone.Last but by no means least, sober people like Sally can begin to pursue purpose and meaning in their lives. Often it starts with active participation in the AA fellowship, and continues or expands to other social service initiatives. For others, sobriety removes the obstacles to activating the talents, purpose and meaning life gave them at birth.

So far, in my 48-year career, I have not encountered any down side to sobriety, nor spiritual life, living harmoniously with one's self, others and the environment.

Each of the four books in this trilogy is an invitation and prescription to action, action based on formulations derived from the experiences and ideas of many, including myself. If you disagree with the formulations, I challenge you to offer alternative ones based on evidence and your experiences. Regardless, it is time to start solving this problem of creating addicts.

ACKNOWLEDGMENTS

I remain eternally grateful to Drina, the love of my life, for continuing to tolerate the unrealistic, but always eventually, fulfilled expectations I set for myself. Without her unwavering support, the expectations would indeed be unrealistic, and the tasks probably never completed.

I am grateful to have known many addicts who allowed me to witness, and to assist them, in their struggle to achieve and maintain sobriety. Of all the accomplishments one can achieve, their success is especially commendable, given from where they start the journey.

I am grateful to the forces that have shaped my never give up character. With this as my foundation, I stubbornly continue to draw attention to the importance of environmental conditions in shaping who we become, and then often stagnate because of siege like conditions.

I am grateful that at this age and stage in life, I am content to creatively synthesize what I know, without the need to garner the testimonials of other professionals in this area of service. The synthesis of many ideas is mine alone, and I take full responsibility for how and what message the work conveys.

I am grateful, however, to two very important people involved in the production of this second, of four, books in the trilogy about addiction. In no particular order of importance, first is my highly competent and reliable word processor and primary editor, Laura Riggs. She is new to the team, and I am very pleased to have her on board. Second, is the superbly competent, reliable and formidable Grant D. Fairley. Tenaciously, he persists in dragging me into today's world of technology and social media, as the essential means by which to tell people about the existence of this, and my other, books. Moreover, without his deft abilities, the books would not be available in print, probably for decades.

Last, but by no means least, I am grateful to know, and to have known, colleagues from all sorts of disciplines and walks of life, who, by example, have modeled the pursuit of meaning and purpose in life. Writing what I believe to be meaningful reflects the influence they have had on me.

ABOUT THE AUTHOR

Alexander T. Polgar, Ph.D., is a tenaciously curious student, consistently motivated to learn the lessons inherent to every experience he encounters. Sally Got Sober is a synthesis of insights gained during many counselling sessions with addicts struggling to overcome obstacles to their abstinence. The book is also a product of his curious mind at work to discern the reasons for the singular efficacy of the Alcoholics Anonymous world wide twelve step program. While his perspectives challenge traditional beliefs as to why twelve step programs work so well, he is the first to champion them as the only source of what addicts need to get, and stay, abstinent from all intoxicants. Fortunately, at his stage and state in life, he is less concerned about challenging orthodoxy and the potential consequences of doing so, than he is with empowering those in need by sharing knowledge that comes from almost five decades of curious inquiry.

REFERENCES

Breggin, P.R. (2008). *Medication madness: The role of psychiatric drugs in cases of violence, suicide and crime.* New York, NY: St. Martin's Griffin.

Coloroso, B. (1994). *Kids are worth it: Giving your child the gift of inner discipline.* Toronto, ON: Somerville House Publishing.

Craika, F., & Bialystokb, E. (2006). Cognition throughout the life span: Mechanisms of change. *Trends in Cognitive Sciences*, *10*(3), 131-8.

Crichton, M. (1988). *Travels.* New York, NY: Ballantine Books.

Drachman, D. (2005). Do we have a brain to spare? *Neurology,* *64*(12), 2004-2005.

Erickson, E. (1998). *The life cycle completed.* New York, NY: W.W. Norton.

F., Dan. (1994). *Sober but stuck: Obstacles most often encountered that keep us from growing in recovery.* Center City, MN: Hazelden Publishing.

Gibbs, J.C. (2003). *Moral development and reality: Beyond*

the theories of Kohlberg and Hoffman. Thousand Oaks, CA: SAGE Publications.

Gladwell, M. (2000). ***The tipping point: How little things can make a big difference.*** New York, NY: Little, Brown.

Hawkins, D.R. (2002). ***Power vs force: The hidden determinants of human behavior***. London, UK: Hay House UK Ltd.

Hoffman, M.L. (2000). ***Empathy and moral development: Implications for caring and justice***. Cambridge, UK: Cambridge University Press.

Kahneman, D. (2011). ***Thinking, fast and slow***. Toronto, ON: Doubleday Canada.

Lickona, T. (1994). ***Raising good children: From birth through the teenage years***. New York, NY: Bantam Books.

Pinker, S. (2018). ***Enlightenment now: The case for reason, science, humanism, and progress***. New York, NY: Viking.

Polgar, A.T. (2019). ***Because we can we must: Achieving the human developmental potential***. Hamilton, ON: Sandriam Publications.

SALLY GETS SOBER AND STARTS TO GROW UP

This second book, of four, in a trilogy about substance abuse tells the story, in the voice of addicted addict Sally, of the challenging journey to getting and staying abstinent from all intoxicants. The message is, that the journey is not easy and that there are several land mines along the way. The first purpose of this tale, therefore, is to warn people like Sally, and those who care about them, of the dangers, and then prepare them to manage successfully this difficult, but extremely rewarding process. The second purpose is to convey that the potential with which Sally, indeed each of us, is born, can only be activated when specific environmental conditions are present, including but certainly not limited to, getting, and staying, sober.

www.ingramcontent.com/pod-product-compliance
Lightning Source LLC
Chambersburg PA
CBHW031448040426
42444CB00007B/1025